THE BRODSWORTH HALL
Chintz

CROSBY STEVENS AND MARY SCHOESER

ENGLISH HERITAGE

First published 2003 by English Heritage

23 Savile Row, London W1S 2ET

Copyright © English Heritage 2003 and Mary Schoeser 2003 (chapters 3 and 4)

Edited by Val Horsler

Designed by Clifford Manlow

Production by Andrew McLaren

Printed by Printco

ISBN 1 85074 863 2

C1.5, 8/03, product code 50772

Contents

Foreword

By Lucinda Lambton

Many years ago, by great good fortune, I was asked to photograph Brodsworth Hall and was to stay within its then crumbling walls, with the frail and funny, sweet and saintly Sylvia Grant Dalton, who lived there for over 70 years.

It is seldom, if ever, that you can say that a house has retained its romance after its owner has died, and it has been restored and opened to the public. This, though, has undoubtedly been the case with this great Northern pile; not only has Brodsworth Hall retained its magic, with the shadows of its history still flitting about the rooms, but wonder of wonders, its beauty has been bettered, with the discovery of a glistening assembly of chintzes, found packed away in cupboards and drawers throughout the house.

With 107 different patterns, this is a treasure trove and half, and what better house than Brodsworth to be found harbouring it. The fashion for chintz was at its peak in the late nineteenth and early twentieth centuries, when it smothered country houses throughout the land; and since there are few houses of that period to have survived as intact as Brodsworth, what more impressive trumpet voluntary of authenticity than to find a neatly packed away, rare-in-its-completeness, collection of chintz? Here is a veritable pattern book of all the uses to which the material could be applied in its heyday; from the shining sweeps on the drawing room's curtains, sofas and chairs, to the humble lining of a bedroom cupboard, Brodsworth is resplendent with the stuff. Most charming of all are the shoe-bag-like pouches that were made to protect each and every one of the tassels hanging from the pelmets on high.

How well I remember wandering through these rooms as they were peeling and crumbling away, whilst despairing of Brodsworth's future. How could it but be disastrous? Who could save such a wreck and, if someone was found, they would surely rob it of life: at best, by the sterile hand of scholarship; at worst, by the creation of some such life-draining horror as a country house hotel or country club. What on earth did the future hold?

Yet now, as if by magic, we are all in that future, with Brodsworth blooming with sympathetic life – its dear old self, but safe from disastrous decay, thanks to English Heritage having led the way with an exemplary restoration that has left the soothing spirit of the place intact.

Never will I forget the sense of being imbued with that spirit, alone in those great dusty rooms; of the icy temperature throughout the house and of the boiling oven-like heat of the lone room in which Sylvia sat, at the end of the long dark corridor, telling me tales such as her courtship by her first husband, Charles Grant Dalton, when he was 30 years old and she was 12 and still in the nursery. Every day his plus-foured figure would peer in at the nursery window. It alarmed her and it alarmed her nanny, who, remonstrating that it was 'not right', in vain implored him to go away. Her parents also failed to put an end to 'his frightening fun' and in the end his was a resounding victory, marrying Sylvia when she was only 15 years old. After his death years later, she married his cousin Eustace. 'He was so kind and so brave, he got into every war he could. He fought in the Boer war, the Kaiser's War and the last war. His first commission was signed by Queen Victoria....When he died he made me promise to look after the house and I have never left it, not for a single day.'

I can still imagine sitting with her tiny form in the great dark dining room, as an old maid tottered round, breaking glasses by the score. As each one smashed, she would round on Sylvia: 'If you had not asked me to come in today, I would not have broken that, would I?' always getting a delighted laugh in return!

Some years later I included Brodsworth in a film on the Great North Road for the BBC, with Sylvia as its enchanting occupant, whizzing about at top speed in her wheelchair through the mirrored maze of statues and pillars, telling the film crew that her plugs were 'roundy goes' (round pins), as well as charming the nation out of its wits with her unselfconscious complaining of 'a scaggy nail...where's the gardener, he's got a lovely thing of shears?' Her reaction to being star of the show was 'I have never known such a carry on in all my bornly days.'

We all felt that we were recording something extraordinary before it vanished forever. Despite Sylvia's brave battle to keep it going, Brodsworth was in a parlous state. I remember noticing with alarm that the pillar capitals of the porte cochère were picturesquely worn away to the size of a wasp's waist.

One night I had been locked out by the alarming nineteenth-century security system by which leaden weighted ropes behind the shutters, when pulled, send impenetrable wooden slatted blinds crashing to the ground. All the downstairs windows are fitted with these contraptions, and there seemed no way of rousing the stone-deaf and one-legged cook. Eventually I managed it, but it took over an hour to so do. It was, though, to be a sleepless night, as Silvia, by then also stone-deaf, was tuned into the World Service at ear-splitting volume. With a sense of the unreal, I found myself in this grand old Yorkshire house, listening to the last hours leading up to President Bhutto's execution in Pakistan, resounding through the great empty rooms at football tannoy pitch.

Silvia never really loved Brodsworth, complaining that 'Those poor cold ladies, the statues, are not quite my gusto I'm afraid. I'm a Georgian. I don't care for the hellish sentimentality of Victorian times.' Many was the time she begged me to 'take away any statuary that you can carry.' Woe to virtuous honesty! Woe too to that honesty in the attics, where dozens of beautiful chairs were on hidden parade; and as a lover of chintz, who knows what would have happened if I had opened the drawers?

Having spent such times in the house, it was of course with greatest apprehension that I returned, years later, after the restoration, dreading the lack of the life that I had so loved. A step through the door, though, and I was immediately engulfed by the old spirit of the place, of that very particular atmosphere of the house having marched through time.

Three details alone were different: my bath was no longer filled to the brim with rubble from the ceiling that had fallen in many years before; there was no longer the aroma of dog's mess – the presence of Silvia's old dog, Binkie, had always hung particularly heavy in the air! – but most wonderful of all the changes to Brodsworth is of course its great collection of chintzes now glistening away throughout the house.

Family Tree of the Thellusson and Grant-Dalton Families

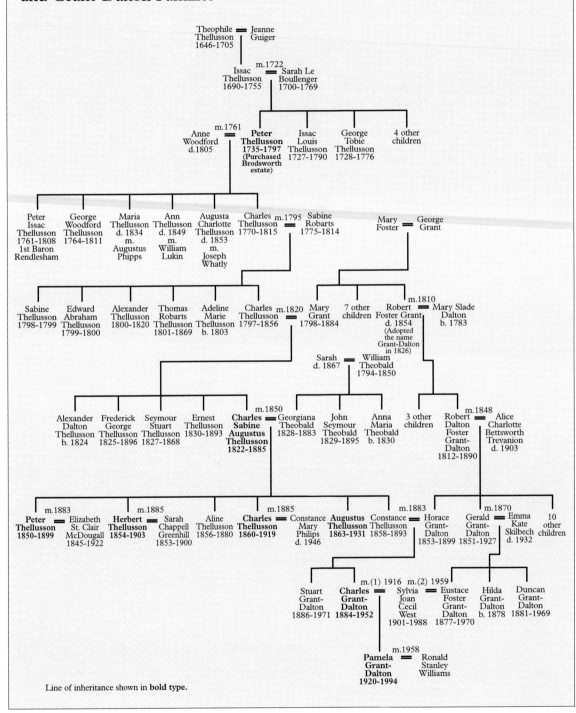

Line of inheritance shown in **bold type**.

Introduction

Chintz was an enormously popular furnishing fabric in later nineteenth- and early twentieth-century Britain. It had many attractions. Light and as smooth as satin, it could be printed with any colour or pattern to suit diverse and ever-changing fashion. Its glazed surface could be dusted and wiped clean. It was sold in a range of qualities and prices from simple roller prints that were very affordable, to complex block-prints that were much more exclusive. Its Indian ancestry gave it associations with the oriental and exotic, and with Empire. And it was a product of the nation's astonishingly successful cotton industry. It was pretty, practical, luxurious and quintessentially English.

Brodsworth Hall in South Yorkshire has a collection of more than 100 designs of printed furnishing textiles, including at least 50 chintzes, all used in the house. This is a rare survival. Chintz was used lavishly both downstairs in reception rooms, and upstairs in family's and servants' bedrooms. It was made into loose covers, fixed upholstery, window curtains and bedhangings. The core of the collection dates to between 1863, when the house was first furnished, and the First World War, although chintz was bought by Sylvia Grant-Dalton, the last member of the family to live at Brodsworth Hall, to the end of the twentieth century. It is a remarkably complete record of the family's acquisitions. We know from bills, inventories and historic photographs that the collection includes examples of most of the patterns bought for the house by three successive generations.

Though many pieces have lost their sheen and crispness through laundering, and are now faded from light, enough survives in good condition to show that these fabrics must originally have had a powerful visual impact. They would have matched in lustre the polished wood, ceramics, glass, gilding, white marble and varnished faux-marbling that fills the house. Many were also brightly coloured with bold motifs. They would have added another layer of strong pattern to rooms already filled with eye-catching ornament.

By the later nineteenth century classic floral chintzes had become associated with a distinctive country house style. Yet despite this association, it is now rare to see large quantities of historic chintz on display in country houses open to the public, especially in reception rooms. There are a number of reasons for this.

The South terrace at Brodsworth at the turn of the century

The Drawing Room showing the silk damask and brocatelle upholstery uncovered; the photograph was taken for the Silver Wedding celebrations of Charles and Constance Thellusson

RIGHT: The Drawing Room in 2003 with a display of covers in 'The Favourite' and 'The Champion Chintz'

A loose cover in the Tournier design chintz used in the Master's and Mistress's bedrooms

Firstly, loose covers were often used to protect more precious and fragile furnishings and took the brunt of damage from light and wear. They were always expected to have a shorter life than the fixed upholstery and when they became worn they were simply replaced. Thus many covers in country house collections, where they survive at all, are shabby and faded and make a disappointing and fragile display. Secondly, chintz covers were often used to give a subtly fashionable flavour to a room with older furniture and decoration. Therefore nineteenth- or twentieth-century sets of loose covers may relate to an interior scheme as it would have appeared for only a brief period in its history. They can therefore be confusing in a period setting. Thirdly, loose covers of course concealed the seat furniture and other upholstery such as cushions. Many historic rooms have understandably been presented to the public in recent years without loose covers in order to show off the primary furnishings, with light and dust kept at bay by

Brodsworth Hall

Brodsworth Hall was built between 1861 and 1863 by Charles Sabine Augustus Thellusson. Charles inherited the Brodsworth estate following a lengthy legal battle over the will of his great-grandfather Peter Thellusson. He demolished an older house on the site and commissioned the little-known London architect Philip Wilkinson to build a new house in a regular, Italianate style. The design was a little old-fashioned for the time, but the house had a modern interior plan and furnishings typical of middle-ranking country houses of the period. It was designed to accommodate Charles, his wife and six children, plus at least 15 indoor servants. Much of the original decoration and contents from 1863 remain in the house today, with a number of alterations and additions by later generations.

What is chintz?

The word 'chintz' is a seventeenth-century Dutch and English version of the Hindi word 'chint' meaning a variegated or spotted cloth. By the mid-nineteenth century chintz referred specifically to a cotton furnishing fabric with a glazed finish. Chintz could refer to a plain cloth in a single colour, but typically chintzes had printed designs. Among the most popular in Britain were three-dimensional floral patterns, often with a white ground. The floral style itself came to be known as chintz, and the term was used to describe, for example, carpets and ceramics. In recent years 'chintzy' has come to mean also pretty but unsubtle, even cheap.

other means. And finally, the chintzes were, in many cases, the second-best fabrics and basically a housekeeping measure. The grandest and often oldest schemes have been exhibited rather than the rooms as they appeared in everyday use.

As a result chintzes have tended to be the poor relations of the fine textiles they protected, and comparatively little attention has been given to their history and display. This is a pity as the chintzes bought for country houses in the later nineteenth and early twentieth century were typically high-quality fabrics. Many processes were involved in making chintz: carving and covering the blocks or making the rollers, preparing the cloth, applying the colourants and other printing chemicals in complex sequences, finishing and glazing. Block printing in particular was highly skilled and the completed fabrics, with their subtle fluctuations in depth of colour and the occasional mis-registration of blocks, are hand-made works of decorative art. Exclusive chintzes of the sort bought for Brodsworth Hall were designed for and manufactured in a small group of élite French and English printing houses. The best of them displayed fine draughtsmanship, balanced colour and harmonious composition, with designs as attuned to nuances of fashion in shade and motif as any couture house.

In the later nineteenth and early twentieth centuries the designs chosen for reception rooms and bedrooms typically sat alongside older decoration and furniture, and they tended to be correspondingly conservative. Most common were naturalistic florals and stripes, with small-scale complementary patterns for lining. They took inspiration from many sources including neoclassicism, English seventeenth-century and French eighteenth-century styles, and Eastern textiles. Nonetheless new artistic forms also made a mark. Chintzes were a channel for the reception of the new leading styles of the later nineteenth century into the homes of the landed classes, albeit in a filtered and unchallenging form. The colours, shapes and subjects favoured by the Aesthetic Movement, the Arts and Crafts Movement and Art Nouveau were echoed and adapted to refresh continually a self-consciously traditional idiom. Thus while a large number of patterns produced for a broadly wealthy market over some 50 years from the 1860s to the 1910s can be grouped together and classed as classic floral chintzes, and successful designs were printed time and again over many decades, there was considerable development in newly drawn designs. There was a discernible shift, for example, from the complex highly-coloured examples of the mid-Victorian period to lighter, more rhythmic Edwardian patterns.

Brodsworth Hall has fine examples of chintzes that were once typical of mainstream Victorian and Edwardian country houses. This book aims first to describe them and to show their place in the furnishing of the house, and then to explore their ancestry. The use of vibrant chintzes in such extravagant quantities emerges as the culmination of a long history of international trade, design development, and evolution in fashions in decoration. Placing the chintz in its physical and historical context offers glimpses of the house in every period of its past, and an understanding of how this collection came to be.

Constance and Herbert Thellusson in the South Hall c1882

A cupboard in the servant's wing filled with chintz covers and curtains, 1991

Plan of Brodsworth Hall

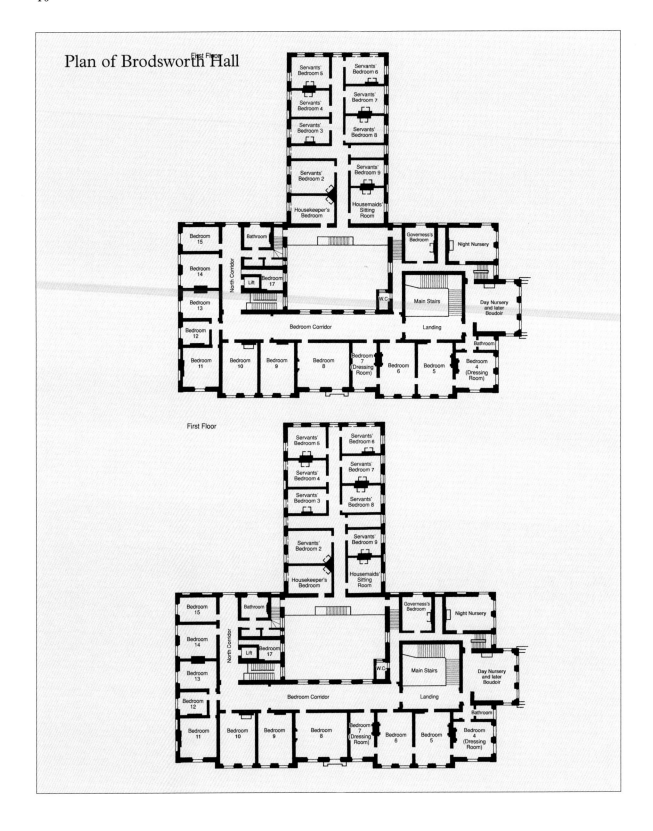

First Floor

The 1863 Chintzes of Brodsworth Hall

Charles Sabine Augustus Thellusson spent over £7,000 in 1863 furnishing the newly-built Brodsworth Hall, and he employed the furnishing company Lapworth Brothers of Bond Street to decorate the house. The interiors were typical of many mid-Victorian houses in bringing together a number of different styles, although unusually they included very little of medieval or Gothic inspiration. The setting was Italianate, while the Drawing Room was largely in eighteenth-century French style and the bedroom furniture was mainly in the comfortable and conservative Grecian style.

Lapworths provided almost all the soft furnishings, using several suppliers but coordinating the choices. As a result there was a pleasing coherence of decoration through the house, despite the range of styles. Generous halls and corridors with crimson star-design carpets, panels of rich painted marbling, and scagliola pillars

The half-tester bed in Grecian style supplied by Lapworths for Bedroom 11

and pilasters unified the ground and first floors. The palette was recognizably mid-Victorian with vivid reds, greens and golds carrying an array of further colours: intense purples, pinks, oranges and blues. The rich colours were punctuated by white marble statues, mirrors and large windows, adding a sense of abundant space and dramatic light. Several pieces of late eighteenth-century, Regency and early Victorian furniture were brought from the earlier, demolished Brodsworth Hall and from a Thellusson house in Brighton, and there were some portraits from the families of both Charles Sabine Thellusson and his wife Georgiana Theobald, as well as a few newly-acquired Dutch 'Old Masters'. These gave a feeling of inherited money, long lineage and educated taste marking a gentlemanly residence.

LEFT: The beginning of the 23-page bill from Lapworths, giving details of the furnishing of Brodsworth Hall in 1863

The textiles supplied for the family side of the house included red and green wool velvets, red silk damask and crimson silk brocatelle for curtains and upholstery. They also included fine Axminster carpets, lace sun curtains, and items such as three embroidered tablecloths, a 'superfine crimson tapestry', and a printed cloth for the dining table. In addition Lapworths supplied 3856 yards of chintz in 19 designs, including seven patterns used for linings. Three designs were used downstairs and the remaining 16 upstairs. They were approximately graduated in price according to the status of the room. The chintzes included examples of both block and roller printing and were a mixture of French and English.

Charles Sabine Thellusson and his wife Georgiana with a baby: probably Peter, 1850

THE GROUND FLOOR

The furniture in most of the rooms on the ground floor of the main block of the house, used by the family, had wool or leather upholstery. However there was silk upholstery in the South Hall and the Drawing Room, and possibly the Library as well: no fixed upholstery from 1863 survives on the Library furniture. Silk was more vulnerable than wool and leather to damage, and so loose covers were needed for everyday use. These were all made from chintz.

THE SOUTH HALL AND DRAWING ROOM

The South Hall was an extended area of hallway adjacent to the Drawing Room used for informal entertaining and music. It was paired with the Drawing Room in decoration. Originally the two rooms had the same cherry red silk damask wall hangings (though these were replaced in the South Hall with gold silk in the early twentieth century). The two rooms also shared a large set of gilded late eighteenth-century settees and armchairs that had come from the old Brodsworth Hall. The settees and chairs were reupholstered in 1863 with fixed covers in a second red damask in a different pattern from that of the wall silk. There were also disparate pieces of older furniture, including a sofa and a large ottoman sociable, which were all upholstered in a third silk: a crimson brocatelle. These too were distributed between the South Hall and the Drawing Room.

Three sets of fitted loose covers were supplied for all this seat furniture. The first set, for when the family was away, was made of plain undyed linen. The remaining two sets were made of chintz and were for everyday use.

It seems the two sets of chintz covers were alternated according to the seasons. The design named 'The Favourite' was probably used in the spring and summer, while 'The Champion Chintz' was used in the autumn and winter. Magnolias which feature in 'The Favourite' are an early summer flower, whereas the foliage in 'The Champion Chintz' is more autumnal. The South Hall was photographed in September 1910 with the covers in 'The Favourite' on the furniture, again suggesting it was the summer design. The South Hall and Drawing Room were the only rooms to have two sets of chintz, doubtless reflecting their importance for entertaining and impressing guests.

One of the gilded settees with the buttoned silk damask upholstery of 1863

Interior of My Boudoir at the old Brodsworth Hall, pencil and watercolour by Anna Louisa Flint, *c*1830. This shows some of the late eighteenth-century gilded furniture that was taken to the new house in 1863. The upholstery, which matched the curtains, may have been chintz

The South Hall *c*1902 with covers in 'The Champion Chintz'

The South Hall 1910 with covers in 'The Favourite'

A tassel and chintz tassel loose cover from the Drawing Room

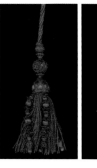

ABOVE, (left to right): Design drawing for 'The Champion Chintz' from which the wooden blocks for printing were cut; one of the gilded settees with a loose cover in 'The Champion Chintz'; design drawing for 'The Favourite'; one of the gilded chairs with a loose cover in 'The Favourite'

The covers were used at least to 1910, and were never replaced as a full set. 'The Champion Chintz' may have been used longer or more often than 'The Favourite' as most of the surviving pieces are in very poor condition. It is probable that the routine of changing covers twice a year, and uncovering the furniture and putting up the silk curtains for formal occasions, had lapsed by the 1920s when housekeeping was simplified for a diminished number of servants. It is also possible that the family simply preferred 'The Champion Chintz'. This may have been because the covers in 'The Favourite' were laundered, probably in the early twentieth century, and given a very stiff and glossy finish. There are several examples of reglazed chintzes in the collection, and these are also very shiny, but the glaze on the pieces in 'The Favourite' is unusually thick.

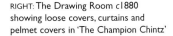

Herbert Thellusson in the South Hall c1882

RIGHT: The Drawing Room c1880 showing loose covers, curtains and pelmet covers in 'The Champion Chintz'

A chamois leather patch inside a loose cover in 'The Favourite' inserted to protect the gilding

The Curtains and Pelmet Covers in the Drawing Room

Lapworths supplied silk curtains and pelmets for the five French windows in the Drawing Room to match the buttoned upholstery on the gilded settees and chairs. It also supplied chintz curtains in both 'The Favourite' and 'The Champion Chintz' to match the loose covers for the furniture. The chintz curtains were light and simple in construction. They were 'bagged', ie the primary fabric and the lining were laid out face together and stitched along the vertical edges, forming a tube which was then turned inside out; the curtain was normally finished with a heading tape and hooks at the top and a hem at the bottom.

The curtains hung on a track below the pelmet in front of blinds and ornate tamboured lace curtains (made by embroidering a chain stitch onto a sheer fabric with a fine hook).

It seems from historic photographs that the pelmets had loose covers too, as well as little individual covers for the tassels that dangle at their lower edge.

THE LIBRARY

Just as the South Hall and Drawing Room were decorated as a pair, the Library and hallways beyond were united by the same chintz loose covers. These were made in a design of entwined ribbons printed in two colourways: one with a green ground, the other with an ochre ground. Green and gold were prominent colours in the Library. The 'Persian design' carpet had a green ground, and the Utrecht velvet curtains were also a vivid green. The wallpaper was gilded and embossed.

The hallway outside the Drawing Room by the Library in 1910, showing loose covers on the seats in both the darker green ground and lighter ochre ground versions of the ribbon design

ABOVE: Details of loose covers in the green ground ribbon design chintz (top left) and the ochre ground (top middle) used in the Library, with (bottom left) the 1842 design drawing

ABOVE RIGHT: The gilded wallpaper in the Library

The Design Drawings

Original design drawings for 14 of the Brodsworth Hall chintzes are held in the Bannister Hall Archive at Stead McAlpin, near Carlisle, part of the John Lewis Partnership. A few of them, including 'The Favourite' and 'The Champion Chintz', have inscriptions naming the pattern. The name was normally assigned by the wholesaler, in this case Walters (later taken over by Warners). Bannister Hall print works operated between about 1798 and 1893 under a series of owners.

The children of Charles Sabine and Georgiana Thellusson, c1870, from a family album

Chintz for the South Hall and Drawing Room in the Lapworths Bill

For Loose Covers for Furniture and Curtain Bags

373 yards Super 4/4 Chintz *	at 2s9d per yd	£51	5s	9d
398 yards " "	at 2s6d per yd	£49	15s	0d
14 Chamois Leathers for Lining	at 2s each	£1	8s	0d
586 yards White Lining	at 10s per yard	£22	8s	4d
4 [rolls?] Crimson Paris Binding	at 36s each	£7	4s	0d
150 yards White glazed Lining	at 10s per yard	£6	5s	0d

* 4/4 refers to the width of the fabric

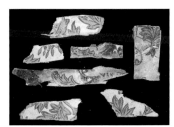

Scraps of wallpaper from the family bedrooms, probably from 1863

The top edge of a window curtain in the lavatera design, showing the heading tape and safety-pin curtain hooks

One of a set of buttoned armchairs supplied by Lapworths in 1863; this one was recovered by Maples in 1886

THE FAMILY BEDROOMS

The bedrooms and dressing rooms of the family were arranged along an L-shaped corridor on the first floor above the reception rooms. Charles Sabine and Georgiana Thellusson had six children to accommodate when the house was finished in 1863. Augustus was a newborn baby, Charles was three years old, and Constance five. The eldest children, Aline, Herbert and Peter were seven, nine and thirteen respectively.

The house was designed with a bedroom and dressing room each for the Master and Mistress and one grand spare room. Although the youngest three children were probably still in the night nursery in 1863, six further bedrooms, with probably two dressing rooms, were undoubtedly intended for the six children. There were also two bathrooms, one adjacent to the Master's Dressing Room, the other at the end of the run of children's bedrooms on the west corridor. It is not known which children used which rooms, though Aline, the eldest daughter, was in Bedroom 9 or 10 in 1880 when a fire broke out associated with her death.

The bedrooms were all decorated in a similar style, less opulent than the reception rooms downstairs, but with solidly made, good quality furniture and moderately expensive furnishings. There seems to have been no distinction between adults and children in the size or type of furniture chosen for rooms along the L-shaped corridor, nor in the patterns of chintz. Nothing redolent of childhood in the decoration survives. Likewise the bedrooms and dressing rooms of male and female members of the family seem to have been very alike.

As in the family rooms downstairs several pieces of furniture for the bedrooms were brought from the old Brodsworth Hall and other Thellusson houses. These included a large set of rosewood side chairs, writing tables, wash stands, a magnificent boat-shaped bed or 'lit en bateau', and probably four other beds as well (the Lapworths bill specified chintz for some beds without supplying the beds themselves). However, the majority of the furniture was supplied new by Lapworths. It included three Spanish mahogany half-tester beds, a single-size boat-shaped bed with upholstered ends, marble-topped washstands, mahogany wardrobes with textile linings, chests of drawers, upholstered armchairs and upholstered side chairs. The walls were probably papered and there were new Brussels carpets in a variety of patterns throughout.

The Master's and Mistress's bedrooms had some furniture evidently covered in the same crimson brocatelle used in the South Hall and Drawing Room. However, almost all the new fixed upholstery in the bedrooms was in chintz, with matching loose covers, window curtains and bed hangings.

The bedroom chintz designs were bright and bold, with dominant reds, greens and purples. The two most expensive fabrics, used in the Master's and Mistress's Bedrooms and a pair of children's bedrooms, were classic mid-Victorian florals: large and elaborate arrangements of flowers including roses. However two further designs, used in the children's bedrooms on the west side, were more sharply in vogue in the 1860s. The first was of delicate posies arranged on vertical purple lace ribbons at a time when lace and the colour purple were very fashionable in dress. The second was of finely drawn flowers and foliage echoing contemporary interest in botanical photography. It seems the fabrics chosen for these slightly lower-status family bedrooms were a little less formal, a little less conservative.

THE SUITE OF BEDROOMS OF THE MASTER AND MISTRESS: BEDROOMS 4 TO 7

A single chintz design was used for these four interconnecting rooms. It was an 1862 block print from the studio of the leading French designer Jean Ulrich Tournier (see chair cover p8). A filling design of posies was printed on a white ground in the centre of the cloth, while a broad richly-coloured floral border was printed down each selvedge edge. Costing 3/6d per yard, it was the most expensive chintz bought for the house, and 445 yards was purchased. All the window curtains and all the loose covers in the suite of rooms were in this design. The lining fabric was in a design imitating green moiré silk.

A bed pole, one of a set of three supplied by Lapworths, possibly for the boat-shaped bed in Bedroom 8, or for Georgiana Thellusson's bed

The Loose Covers
The chintz loose covers for the furniture in the Master's and Mistress's bedrooms had white glazed linen linings. The main seams of the covers were machine stitched, but many yards of decorative red binding tape were sewn by hand in tiny running stitch.

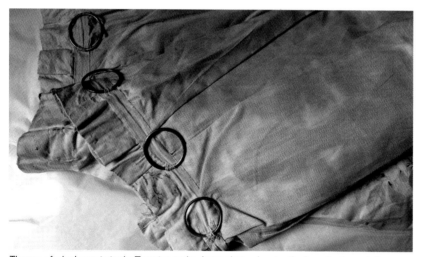

The top of a bed curtain in the Tournier studio design chintz, showing the box pleating and rings, with a lining in a green moiré design. The curtain was probably one of a pair hung over poles to form a canopy above Georgiana Thellusson's bed.

A detail of the chintz lining in one of the wardrobes supplied by Lapworths

Sylvia Grant-Dalton's bed as it appeared in her later years. The cover on the headboard and the curtains are different Edwardian chintzes. The poles are post-1863 but may echo the original arrangement

Chintz for the Bedrooms of the Master and Mistress in the Lapworths bill

Superfine White ground French chintz				
Containing 445 yards	at 3s6d per yard	£77	17s	6d
Green Watered lining for ditto				
Containing 380 yards	at 1s3d per yard	£23	15s	0d
24 yards White Lining	at 10s per yard	£1	0s	0d
302 yards Paris Binding	at 4d per yard	£5	0s	8d
67 yards fine Twine Fringe	at 2s6d per yard	£8	7s	6d
16 Silk and Worsted Curtain Holders	at 11s each	£8	16s	0d

THE PRINCIPAL GUEST ROOM, BEDROOM 8

Bedroom 8 was the largest of the bedrooms. It had a fine veneered boat-shaped bed, probably from the 1850s, with three brass poles to support a pair of large chintz curtains. Although a grand room, undoubtedly intended to impress visitors, it had a relatively inexpensive chintz at 1/10d a yard. The Lapworths bill of 1863 describes it as a 'superfine chintz' with a green lining. No design matching this description survives in the collection.

Detail of a loose cover in the rose and phlox design chintz used in Bedrooms 9 and 10, with (far right) the 1861 design drawing for this design

BEDROOMS 9 AND 10

Bedrooms 9 and 10 were furnished as a pair, using a Bannister Hall print. The design was of block-printed roses and phlox on a roller-printed ground of purple stars. At 2/9d a yard it was as expensive as 'The Champion Chintz' used in the South Hall and Drawing Room. The lining was of purple stars.

It seems Lapworths supplied a half-tester bed for one of these rooms, but the bed in the other room was older. The bed hangings alone in the two rooms needed 129 yards of chintz, suggesting that the second, older bed had particularly extensive or elaborate hangings. The two bedrooms also had 'toilet draperies', requiring 24 yards of chintz and 61 yards of lining. These were probably dressing tables covered in chintz, though none survives to show the style.

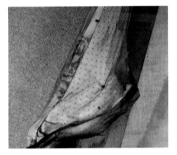

Detail of the backboard of a half-tester bed from Bedroom 9 or 10, showing layers of chintz including a design of purple stars that complemented the ground of the rose and phlox design

BEDROOMS 11, 12 AND 13

These three rooms were all called bedrooms in the Lapworths bill, though the middle and smallest room was probably used as a dressing room. They were decorated as a set using a French roller-printed chintz in a design of lavatera. The design was printed in grey, purple and copper on a grey geometric ground. At 2/- a yard it was moderately expensive. The associated lining was a scroll design described as 'drab' in the 1863 bill. Surviving pieces are grey, though it is possible that the original brownish colours have completely faded. Certainly all the dyes except the grey on the main chintz were very fugitive, both in washing and light.

RIGHT: A detail of an unfaded piece of the lavatera design chintz on an upholstered bed end from Bedroom 13; the document for the design, dated 1863, is held at the Musée de L'Impression sur Étoffes at Mulhouse in France; (middle) a detail of a faded curtain in the lavatera design chintz; (right) a detail of the lining to one of the curtains in the lavatera design chintz

Synthetic Dyes

Dye analysis has indicated early synthetic purple and pink dyes in the chintzes from Brodsworth Hall. The first analine dye, derived from coal tar, was mauveine discovered by William Perkin in 1856. It proved extremely popular and a voracious demand for brightly coloured textiles ensued. Many new dyes came onto the market although the science was still at an experimental stage. The best of the new dyes were very stable but the worst were hopelessly fugitive in light and washing.

BEDROOMS 14 AND 15

The final two bedrooms on the west side of the family corridor were decorated with a third French chintz. The design was of vertical twisted strips of grey and purple lace with posies in bright green, pink and purple. Again very unstable dyes were used and there was severe fading. The 1863 bill describes a lilac spot lining but no example of the lining survives.

THE BATHROOM AND BEDROOM 17

The bathroom off the short corridor opposite Bedroom 14 was decorated to match the remaining bedroom (probably used as a dressing room) into which the lift was later inserted. These two rooms were given a fourth French chintz at 2/- a yard. The lining was a green chintz in a design imitating moiré silk (at 15d a yard, it was cheaper than the lining of similar design used in the Master's and Mistress' Bedrooms). No example remains in the collection. A charge was made for an upholsterer's time 'making up and oil-proofing' chintz for the bathroom, indicating that it was treated to make it waterproof.

THE BEDROOM CORRIDOR

The corridor that ran beside the family bedrooms was a broad, light circulating space. Much of the older furniture belonging to the family found a place there and the corridor was densely furnished in 1863. The seat furniture probably included a large early nineteenth-century banquette, or low sofa, from one of the other Thellusson houses, which Lapworths divided into two. The two halves are still in the collection, on the landing at the top of the main staircase rising from the Entrance Hall. There is no mention in the 1863 bill of loose covers for the divided banquette, although they were covered in crimson silk brocatelle and so it is very likely they did have loose covers.

Originally there were two of these large banquettes. The second one was left complete. Like the divided banquette, it had fixed upholstery in the brocatelle used on some of the furniture downstairs. It was mentioned in the inventory taken in 1885 after the death of Charles Sabine Thellusson. By then it was in the bedroom corridor, but it may originally have been downstairs, possibly outside the Library. The bill shows that the chintz bought for the banquette was the same price as the

FAR LEFT: A section of buttoned upholstery in the lace design chintz showing the original vibrant colours, with, next to it, a faded loose cover in the same chintz

LEFT: Constance Thellusson in Bedroom 14 *c*1882, seated on an armchair with a loose cover in the lace design chintz (already faded by this date) next to a side chair with a matching loose cover

BELOW: The cover on this armchair, supplied by Lapworths and still in the Brodsworth Hall collection, may be the one shown in the photograph of Constance

A detail of the loose cover for the undivided banquette in an unglazed cretonne; the design is from *c*1840 but this is probably a later reprint

LEFT: A detail of a chair seat cover in the chintz used also to patch the undivided banquette cover, with the 1854 design drawing by J Mansbendel; the piece is probably a later reprint

Library ribbon design chintz at 2/2d per yard, and it is listed in the bill after the Library chintz. The bill specifies 21½ yards of chintz for a twelve-foot settle in the Hall. It describes the chintz by its ground but the writing is unfortunately difficult to read. It may say 'marne' meaning marled or spotted.

The only covers that survive for the divided banquette are probably twentieth-century, but one earlier cover does survive for the undivided banquette. It is in poor condition, made up of a heavy unglazed printed cotton fabric patched extensively with chintz, possibly part of a curtain. The design is by J Mansbendel, dating to 1854. Evidence from a surviving loose cover in the design suggests that it, too, was a later reprint bought after 1863. The loose cover is for the seat of one of the set of rosewood side chairs brought from an older Thellusson house. These chairs were reupholstered several times and at some point between 1863 and 1886 pins were inserted in the frames to hold the drop-on seats in position. The cover in the Mansbendel chintz has holes to accommodate the pins, suggesting it is post-1863. This undivided banquette cover does not match the description in the Lapworths bill. It is not chintz, and it has a white ground. The design is dated to *c*1840, which is early enough to be supplied by Lapworths, but the fabric may well be a later reprint.

A trunk covered in Brussels carpet and lined with a two-tone madder dyed chintz

THE BEDROOMS OF THE CHILDREN AND SERVANTS

In addition to the 16 chintz designs used along the family bedroom corridor, a further five designs were bought in 1863 for the bedroom of the governess, the children's night nursery and the bedrooms of the higher female servants. Chintzes may have been used to furnish the bedrooms of the other female and male servants as well, but no record survives. Cheaper fabrics may well have been bought for these rooms, possibly made up locally or by the servants themselves.

THE NIGHT NURSERY

The Night Nursery was furnished mainly with a wool damask used also in the Day Nursery and the Schoolroom. However the Lapworths bill also charged for 3yds of chintz to cover a basket. This may have been a blanket box or linen basket, but it may equally have been a cot or bassinette. Three brass bed poles were bought at the same time, possibly to drape curtains over the beds of Augustus, Charles and Constance.

THE BEDROOM OF THE GOVERNESS

A bedroom next to the Night Nursery was reserved for the governess. It appears to have been furnished in a similar style to the family bedrooms. It had a 'set of Chintz Curtains, Bed Vallances etc' in a moderately expensive chintz at 2/3d a yard, with a green trellis design lining at 10d a yard. However the design has not been identified in the collection.

Details of two unlined valances, possibly used on servants' beds in the later nineteenth century

THE BEDROOMS OF THE FEMALE SERVANTS

Lapworths supplied chintz for three bedrooms on the first floor of the servant's wing used by the housekeeper and ladies' maids, three of the higher ranking servants. The 1863 bill mentions 91yds of French chintz at 1/8d a yard, plus three linings: a trellis design lining at 11d a yard, a green trellis design lining at 8d a yard and a pink lining at 10½d a yard. Again both the window curtains and the bed furniture were in chintz. The style of the beds is not known, though one mahogany bed pole was purchased, presumably for draped bed curtains. No chintzes matching the description in the bill survive.

The Later Chintzes of Brodsworth Hall

②

While 'The Favourite' and 'The Champion Chintz' remained in use at least to 1910 and probably beyond the First World War, all the other 1863 chintzes in the family rooms were replaced at least once before the 1920s. New loose

covers, bed hangings and window curtains were bought as the older sets became faded and worn or fell out of fashion. Indeed, there were as many printed textiles in use at the end of the Edwardian period as in 1863. Chintz was still the most frequent choice, though a few cretonnes (unglazed, heavier cottons and linens) were introduced as well. Classic florals persisted among the new purchases, drawn and coloured to suit current mainstream fashion, and the influence of French revival styles continued. However, there were also a few more adventurous additions introducing a flavour of Art Nouveau, and touches of chinoiserie and Arts and Crafts styles.

Each of Charles Thellusson's four sons inherited the house in turn, but none produced an heir. In 1931 Brodsworth Hall passed to Charles Grant-Dalton, the younger son of Constance Thellusson, sister of the four sons. He and his wife Sylvia had a daughter, Pamela, and it was she who eventually passed the house to English Heritage in 1990. Charles Grant-Dalton died in 1952, leaving Brodsworth Hall to Pamela but making provision for her mother to live there for life. Seven years later Sylvia married Eustace Grant-Dalton, a cousin of her first husband. Eustace died in 1970, and Sylvia lived at Brodsworth Hall until her death in 1988 at the age of 87.

LEFT: Sylvia and Charles Grant-Dalton on their wedding day

Sylvia and Eustace Grant-Dalton

1864–1885: CHARLES THELLUSSON

The decorative schemes at Brodsworth Hall changed little in the 20 years after the first furnishing by Lapworth Brothers. However, Charles Thellusson did make a few further purchases, adding new loose covers and curtains in both chintz and cretonne, and refurnishing two of the bedrooms of his children.

RIGHT: A detail of a loose cover in a design of sprigs of roses with trailing ferns, used in Bedroom 9 after the death of Aline Thellusson, with (middle) the 1871 design drawing for this design; (far right) a detail of the backboard from the Bedroom 9 half-tester bed, showing the layers of fabric, including the pink woven moiré design that was used as a lining to the chintz in a design of sprigs of roses with trailing ferns

A detail of a quilted loose cover for a chair of c1880 for possibly Aline Thellusson's bedroom with laundry marks inside include 'reglazed'

A detail of the yew stems design chintz used to cover over the lavatera design on the boat-shaped bed from Bedroom 13; the pattern is block printed on a roller printed ground designed to look like a fine twill

BEDROOM 9

Aline Thellusson died in 1880 following a fire in her bedroom, probably Bedroom 9. Mawes of Doncaster refurbished the room, renovating and reupholstering the furniture damaged by fire, water and smoke, and supplying new loose covers and curtains. The chintz chosen was a classic design of sprigs of roses with trailing ferns.

BEDROOM 13

The lace design chintz in Bedroom 13 seems to have been replaced at some point before 1886 with a chintz in a design of yew stems, heather and small flowers. A bed with upholstered ends from Bedroom 13 has this design covering the 1863 lavatera design, indicating the order of furnishing. Loose covers in the yew stem design were made for chairs in the rosewood set with drop-on seats that were altered prior to 1886. These loose covers have no holes for pins and so can be assumed to be earlier than 1886. The reason for refurnishing Bedroom 13 is not known.

Constance Thellusson c1882 with her copy of a Dutch painting that hung in the Dining Room; beside her is one of the bedroom rosewood side chairs with a loose cover in the rose and phlox design used in Bedrooms 9 and 10

It is possible that Charles Thellusson refurbished other family rooms as well, and at least one other chintz of about this date survives in the collection. However, two photographs from c1882, only three years before Charles died, suggest that he made few changes in the bedrooms. The first picture (p19) is of Constance, his daughter, seated in Bedroom 14. This photograph shows a mahogany side chair and an armchair still with loose covers in the 1863 lace design. The second photograph (opposite) is again of Constance, standing by an easel with a rosewood side chair. This chair also still has its 1863 loose cover, in the design of phlox and roses used in Bedrooms 9 and 10. At least two of the bedroom chintzes were clearly still in use towards the end of Charles Thellusson's life.

1885–1899: PETER THELLUSSON

Peter Thellusson, Charles's eldest son, inherited Brodsworth Hall in 1885. He carried out extensive repairs to the building and undertook some redecoration. In 1886 he employed the fashionable firm Maples of London to supply fabrics and reupholster furniture in several of the family bedrooms. His taste in chintz was much like his father's, though a few of the individual printed fabrics he introduced were more adventurous choices.

A portrait of Peter Thellusson painted by George Percy Jacomb Hood c1885–95, hanging in the billiard room

LEFT: The back of an armchair upholstered in an unglazed printed fabric of c1870–80, probably French

THE SUITE OF BEDROOMS OF THE MASTER AND MISTRESS, BEDROOMS 4 TO 7

Maples supplied two fabrics for this suite. The first was a chintz in a bold magnolia design with a green ground for the Mistress's rooms. The second, for the Master's rooms, was a rose print on a soft woven self-textured ground, described in the Maples bill as a dimity. The two fabrics had chintz linings in the same design but different colourways.

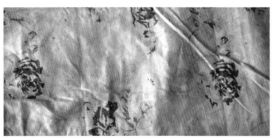

FAR LEFT: A detail of a chintz loose cover in a design of c1850, reprinted and supplied by Maples in 1886, used in the Mistress's Bedroom and Dressing Room

LEFT: A detail of a curtain in a design of roses printed onto a fabric with a woven design of birds and flowers, described in the Maples bill as a dimity, used in the Master's Bedroom and Dressing Room

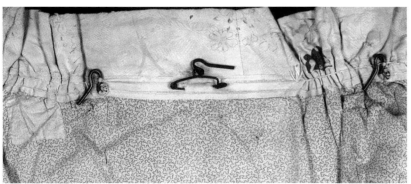

The top edge of one of the dimity window curtains. The construction is very similar to that of the curtains supplied by Lapworths 25 years earlier: the curtain is bagged, the top is simply gathered and there is a double-channelled heading tape. The original hooks may have been the safety-pin style ones, though long-shanked ones are found on several of the later nineteenth-century curtains in the collection

BEDROOM 14

Bedroom 14 was also refurbished by Maples in 1886, using a chintz in a design of trailing wild roses. The complementary lining design was of the roller printed ground only, a design of small brown parallel slashes. It is not known why Bedroom 14 was chosen for redecoration.

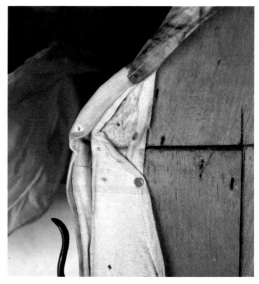

ABOVE LEFT: The trailing wild roses design supplied by Maples in 1886, with (beneath it) the 1873 design drawing and (middle) a mahogany side chair with a drop-on seat in this design

ABOVE RIGHT: A detail of the backboard of the half-tester bed from Bedroom 14, showing the brown slash design that was the complementary fabric to the trailing wild rose design below the top cover: an arborescent design cretonne of *c*1900

ABOVE: A detail of a chair seat reupholstered by Maples in 1886, in a design of 1848 called 'The False Acacia'

RIGHT: The half-tester bed in Bedroom 14 as it was in Sylvia Grant-Dalton's later years. The cretonne on the bed was first produced by Ramm, Son and Crocker at the turn of the century, and was in production as a screen print in the 1990s

1899–1919: HERBERT AND CHARLES THELLUSSON

Herbert Thellusson succeeded his brother Peter in 1899, but lived only to 1903. He appears to have made few changes to the house in that time. In contrast, Charles, the third son, who inherited next, refreshed the decoration throughout the house. This activity was made possible by substantial new income from Brodsworth colliery.

Chintz was still the most common choice for the bedrooms, though the Library and at least two bedrooms had new furnishings in printed cretonne. The primary designs, excluding the linings, were all high-quality block-prints and, like the 1863 chintzes, a mixture of French and English. The basic palette of red, green and purple persisted, though the colours tended to be paler and the treatment of the floral subjects was softer and looser than in the earlier, Victorian designs. As in previous years a few pieces were bolder and more sharply contemporary, notably one chintz chair cover in a design inspired by Art Nouveau, and another depicting fashionable chrysanthemums.

Detail of a loose cover for a bolster in a cretonne of c1890, probably used on a sofa

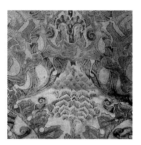

FAR LEFT: A detail of later nineteenth-century chair cover in an unglazed fabric inspied by chinoiserie; (middle) a detail of a loose cover in a chintz first printed in 1890; chrysanthemums were associated with the orient and were fashionable at the turn of the century; (right) a detail of a loose cover in a chintz of c1900, in a fluid, curvilinear Art Nouveau style

LEFT: The Library in 1910 showing the loose covers in a rose design cretonne (above), supplied by Hall and Armitage of Wakefield in 1904

ABOVE: A detail of a chintz loose cover in a design of rose buds of c1900 used in Bedroom 11, with next to it the design drawing of the 1852 design, reprinted by Le Behrins in France in 1900; a detail of a piece of chintz in a design of vertical ribbons and bunches of daisies, with next to it the design drawing, first printed in France c1890

A chintz tie-back in the design of garlands of purple flowers

A detail of a chintz cushion in the design of garlands of purple flowers supplied for the Principal Guest Room, Bedroom 8, in 1904

A detail of the carpet from Bedroom 8 supplied by Hall and Armitage in 1904

The Principal Guest Room, Bedroom 8 in 1990, showing the wall brackets for the three brass poles that supported the chintz bed curtains over the boat-shaped bed

THE PRINCIPAL GUEST ROOM, BEDROOM 8

Charles Thellusson entertained lavishly at Brodsworth Hall, and he completely redecorated Bedroom 8 for guests. Hall and Armitage of Wakefield repainted the woodwork including the doors, skirtings, shutters and curtain poles, in a fashionable ivory. They repapered the walls in a pale sparkling mica paper with a frieze of wisteria, and supplied a new carpet in a vigorous design of large scrolls and stylised flowers in orange, grey and aqua. And they provided new chintz, in a flowing and impressionistic design of garlands of purple flowers with green ribbons and bows. As in 1863, the chintz was used for window curtains and for loose covers for chairs and cushions. It was also used for two vast bed curtains, measuring 3700mm by 3200mm, draped over three brass poles above the boat-shaped bed. The redecoration made the room much lighter and, particularly through the carpet, gave it a loosely Art Nouveau style. The final effect was emphatically modern and very sumptuous.

THE BOUDOIR

The large room to the north of the Master's and Mistress's suite of bedrooms had been used as a Day Nursery while the Thellusson children were young. However by 1885, in the absence of children, it was used as the Mistress's sitting room or boudoir. The 1885 inventory listed crimson damask curtains in the windows, probably still the red wool damask supplied by Lapworths. These curtains were replaced, probably around 1900, by chintz in a design of open roses.

LEFT: Sylvia Grant-Dalton on one of the sofas in the Boudoir with a loose cover in a design of poppies c1890 (a detail is shown below); the glaze appears very stiff and shiny. The curtain is in a design of large open roses of c1880-1900 (detail above)

LEFT: Sylvia Grant-Dalton in the Boudoir in fancy dress. The chintz curtains of c1880–1900 are in the design of large open roses

LEFT: A view of the Boudoir, mid-twentieth century, showing the chintz curtains with broad ribbon tiebacks

BELOW: The top of the curtain in the Boudoir had fine pleats and a white heading tape with short-shanked hooks.

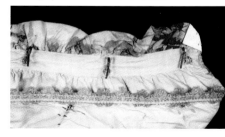

RIGHT: A detail of a cushion cover in an unglazed fabric printed with a design imitating an ikat weave

FAR RIGHT: A detail of a chair cover in an unglazed fabric with a design in a naïve style indebted to the Arts and Crafts movement and oriental designs

1919–1931: AUGUSTUS THELLUSSON

Augustus Thellusson, Charles's youngest son and the last of the sons to inherit Brodsworth Hall, probably visited the house no more than once a year in the 1920s, for the shooting. He never married and his main residence was at Broadstairs in Kent. He appears to have added no chintzes, although a few cushions, loose covers and curtains in unglazed fabrics probably date to his occupancy.

1931–1988: THE GRANT-DALTON FAMILY

Charles and Sylvia Grant-Dalton made many changes to the house to modernise it and make it more comfortable, including altering fireplaces, installing washbasins in the bedrooms and redecorating walls. They also added some furnishing fabrics upstairs, including plain green curtains and bed hangings, and a number of printed textiles.

They seem to have liked classic floral chintzes, in line with the resurgence of chintz in country houses in the 1930s. However, a diminished income dictated retrenchment and the older chintzes were kept in use. Because several sets of covers had been made for most of the family rooms over the years, and much of the seat furniture had been supplied in sets so that covers fitted several chairs, it was possible to bring stored chintzes back out, and to mix up the designs using the best pieces.

TOP LEFT: Detail of a cushion cover in an unglazed fabric in a design of branches, leaves and fanciful flowers derived from crewel work, produced by Warner Fabrics, 1939

TOP RIGHT: A detail of a curtain in an unglazed fabric in a naïve 'Jacobethan' style, printed for Warner fabrics between 1930 and 1940 when the blocks were destroyed

ABOVE LEFT: A detail of a chintz curtain in a design of roses, tulips and other flowers and foliage, issued for export by Sandersons in 1941, but appearing in the home trade price list for 1952

ABOVE RIGHT: A detail of a chintz chair cover in a design of roses on a lace ground, probably a later twentieth-century revival of a later nineteenth century design

RIGHT: Bedroom 10, no longer used by the family as it appeared in 1991

Sylvia Grant-Dalton continued to reupholster furniture and to buy fabrics for loose covers to the end of her life. She had the gilt chairs in the South Hall recovered in a gold cotton damask, and the chairs in the same set in the Drawing Room covered in a heavy printed cotton with a pink foliate design. And although the Lapworths covers in 'The Favourite' and 'The Champion Chintz' were no longer used, she had new loose covers made for the gilt settees and the ottoman sociable in the centre of the Drawing Room, which retained their 1863 silk damask and brocatelle upholstery.

Gradually fewer and fewer rooms were used. Bedroom 8, the Principal Guest Room, was one of the first to be abandoned. Its 1904 carpet and some of the curtains were moved to the suite of Master's and Mistress's bedrooms. Likewise, by 1988 Bedroom 10 contained a brass bed with no mattress and the backboard of an unrelated half-tester bed, covered in the 1904 rose design.

By the end of her life Sylvia Grant-Dalton had only a few staff and she struggled to look after the house. There was mining subsidence and a leaking roof, and the fragile interiors suffered from damp and insect infestation. Most of the chintzes that were still in use in 1988 were degraded and threadbare, though many more in excellent condition were still stored in cupboards and concealed below layers of fixed upholstery on the furniture.

One of the eighteenth-century gilded settees with a loose cover as used by Sylvia Grant-Dalton

A detail of the backboard on Sylvia Grant-Dalton's bed, showing the first fixed cover and two subsequent loose covers

Sylvia Grant-Dalton's bed

A hamster on a chintz-covered chair in the Master's Dressing Room, Bedroom 4, mid-twentieth century; the curtains in the background are the cut-down Drawing Room curtains in 'The Favourite'

The Layers of Chintz on Furniture at Brodsworth Hall

In many cases a loose cover in better condition was simply placed over the top of one or more damaged covers, creating several layers of different fabrics. For example, by 1988 the headboard on the bed in the Mistress's bedroom, Bedroom 6, had three layers of covers. The first layer, lying nearest to the wooden structure, was a chintz in a small-scale design in red. This was probably the first covering supplied with the bed in 1863. The second layer was a green rep loose cover probably dating to the 1930s, which was left in place when another loose cover, the final layer, was put on. This top loose cover is in a rose design, probably Edwardian, and it was doubtless brought out of store in Mrs Grant-Dalton's later years. The curtains on the bed, which originally hung on a half-tester bed rather than over poles, were in another rose design, dating to 1904.

ABOVE: The South Hall in 2003 showing the loose covers in the reproduction of 'The Favourite', made to protect the fragile silk damask upholstery

AFTER 1990: ENGLISH HERITAGE

English Heritage took over Brodsworth Hall in 1990, and since then the collections have been gradually researched, catalogued and displayed.

Many of the chintzes have needed specialist textile conservation having suffered in the past from light, dirt, laundering, wear and storage on wooden shelves. Several methods have been adopted. Where possible, the chintzes have been cleaned to remove disfiguring and damaging dirt. Tears and weak areas have been strengthened using a variety of techniques including covering with a fine net and stitching and adhering to support fabrics. In addition, a new housekeeping regime has been developed. Echoing Victorian and Edwardian practice, there is meticulous management of dust and light, and plain cotton covers are placed over the furniture when the house is closed in the winter.

The Reproduction of 'The Favourite'
'The Favourite' has been reproduced to make loose covers to protect the silk-covered settees in the South Hall, and to make curtains for the suite of bedrooms of the Master and Mistress, copying pieces in the collection.

May Berkouwer, Textile Conservator, cleaning the tassel covers in 'The Favourite'

A textile conservator vacuum cleaning one of the gilded settees

The Brodsworth Hall chintz collection is a remarkable testament to the vitality of chintz in a country house over 140 years. It is a unique record of the history of furnishing by a single family, mixing old with new, and adapting a house to suit the needs and tastes of three generations. The collection offers an authentic source for the continued inspiration and enjoyment of visitors.

Stephanie Rawkins preparing the positives for making screens to print 'The Favourite'

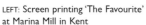

LEFT: Screen printing 'The Favourite' at Marina Mill in Kent

The cleaning of a loose cover in the 1904 design for the Principal Guest Room, Bedroom 8

BELOW: Tiebacks for the bedroom curtains made probably in the 1940s from the Drawing Room curtains in 'The Favourite'; light and acidity from the interlining have badly damaged the chintz

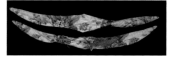

LEFT: The Master's Dressing Room, Bedroom 4, in 2003 with reproduction curtains in 'The Favourite'

The History of Chintz

③

Today the word 'chintz' is inextricably linked to the nineteenth-century English country house style, but its making is documented at least 1000 years earlier, when washable block-printed and hand-painted Indian cottons were already an essential aspect of the trade routes that linked the eastern Mediterranean to the Far East. Surviving examples found in Egypt and Indonesia, and radiocarbon-dated to the thirteenth and fourteenth centuries respectively, are the earliest printed cottons to illustrate combinations of blues, reds and black in the same cloth. It is this multi-coloured feature (rather than the earlier patterns dyed in a single-colour, typically indigo blue) that came to be associated with the meaning of 'chintz' in the West, to such an extent that patterns produced in a limited palette were called 'demi-chintzes' by late eighteenth- and early nineteenth-century British printers, while 'chintzing' was used by weavers such as those in Macclesfield and Yorkshire to denote the addition of extra coloured wefts (a meaning still current today). It was not until the 1840s or 1850s that a particular style began to be associated with the term and even later, it seems, that it also came to denote a highly-glazed finish, even on an unpatterned cloth.

Radiocarbon dated to 1300–1380, this cotton ceremonial banner illustrates the early date by which printers and dyers of the Indian subcontinent had already developed complex skills. It was made in Gujurat for the Indonesian market and is hand painted with resists against the indigo blues and a mordant for the red.

The multi-faceted nature of the term itself is indicative of the complexity of its manufacture and the circuitous trading routes by which chintzes reached Europe. Thought to have originated from the Sanskrit *chitta* (also *chitra*, meaning variegated), by the time European merchant-adventurers reached India's western ports in the 1500s numerous derivations were in use, including the Hindi *chint* and Gujarati *chit*. The first westerners to arrive were the Portuguese, who took *chita* with them to the Malay Archipelago, where they captured the port of Malacca in 1511. Such cloths were an essential element in the complex bartering systems used to obtain spices in these islands (the former East Indies, or 'Spice Islands'). Along with pepper, cloves, nutmeg and mace, which remained the primary cargo on westward-bound ships for over a century more, some cottons made the journey too. As early as 1508 a church in Lisbon contained Indian

The 'simplest' of Indian chintzes – or multi-coloured cotton cloths – were dyed in at least two colours. These were normally indigo and a madder root-type red dye, often chay. The first had to be patterned by drawing a paste on the cloth to resist the dye, while the second required drawing with a mordant to bind the dye to the fibre.

cottons originating from both Cambay in the north-west and Calicut, on India's south-western shores. The latter source gave rise to the term 'calico', which was to become the generic term for cotton cloths '...of different kinds, plain, printed, stained, dyed, chintz, muslins and the like'. This was Thomas Sheraton's description of calico, given in his *Encyclopedia* of 1804–7, by which date Britain was becoming the foremost source of printed calicos, wresting from India a position that not long before had appeared unassailable.

By the early 1900s smaller-patterned highly-glazed cottons were often called 'Manchester chintzes' after the distribution centre for Lancashire's many roller printed cloths, which were lower in price than block printed chintzes and intended for middle class homes. These patterns, marketed by Warner & Sons, reflect the then-current taste for neo-Regency interiors.

The Indian expertise with cotton derived in part from their long experience with this fibre, which has never been a European crop. The most difficult of the principal natural fibres to spin (the others being wool, silk and flax, the latter making linen), cotton is also second only to linen in its resistance to dyes. Producing a fast-to-washing, solid-coloured or pattern-dyed cotton required the application of a mordant, a solution containing a mineral salt or metallic oxide capable of bonding cotton and certain dyes – especially the pinks, reds, browns, purples and blacks created from alizarin-rich roots of plants such as madder and chay. A morsel of mordant-dyed red cotton estimated to be about 4000 years old has been unearthed at Mohenjo Daro in the Indus Valley (modern-day Pakistan), attesting to the antiquity of such skills in this region. But the chintzes for which the Indian subcontinent became famed required much more than the use of a single mordant. A series of treatments repeated the application of a different mordant for each colour to be obtained in this way: alum for red, iron for black and a mixture of the two for purples and browns. Blue required an entirely different process since it was obtained from indigo, a photosensitive dye that develops its colour only after the dye-soaked cloth contacts the air. As a result, areas not to be blue had to be completely covered with a wax or mud paste – a 'resist' – to prevent penetration of the dye. Often, more than one dye was used to create a single colour. For example, chay with the mordant alum produced a bright red, but where the cloth had also been applied with sappenwood (an Asian dyewood with mordanting qualities) the same chay dye-bath turned those areas dark red. A mordant for yellow dye placed on areas of blue created green once immersed in a yellow dyebath, and was also overlaid on red and purple to similarly modify these colours.

All the mordant and resist patterning was drawn on, using a pen-like instrument with a fibrous egg-shaped reservoir bound near its tip. Called a *qalam*, it is still used in Kalahasti in southern Andhra Pradesh, one of several centuries-old textile centres along India's eastern Coromandel Coast that contributed to the renown of this region's *kalamkari* (from the Persian and literally 'pen workmanship'). *Kalamkari*, which were painted on both sides, were also produced in Surat, not far from Cambay, but in this region the pattern's outlines were often marked out with charcoal-laden blocks. In either case these were referred to as 'painted' (or, in Portuguese, *pintado*) and the cloth had first to be beaten smooth to provide a crisp surface that would preserve the delicate lines of the pattern. Herein lay the origins of the finishing process. The final glazing might similarly be the result of pressure alone, or it could be provided by buffing the surface with rice paste, egg albumen or starch, or it need not be applied at all. The resulting cotton cloths – visually sophisticated, technically complex, brilliantly coloured and yet washable – were rarities in Europe, being occasionally traded through the French free port of Marseilles in the 1570s and 1580s and as early as the 1560s carried northward from Lisbon by the Dutch, who were establishing their own 'spice route' merchant-mariners during the same period. By these routes came the calicoes recorded in the port city of Southampton between 1559 and 1573. In England in 1600 *pintado* became available directly from the

Vivid red backgrounds were typical of many Indian chintzes and highly prized in the 'Spice Islands', where they were used as currency. They were sometimes also traded in Europe, especially by mariners from the Low Countries, where this example was found. It probably dates from the 1640s or 1650s, but may have been made as much as 100 years later.

Like *kalamkari*, the word *palampore* is derived from *qalam*, the pen-like instrument used on the subcontinent to draw patterns on cloth, but in England it was used to describe large panels with a border and an upright design, often a tree of life. The delicate workmanship typical of *palampores* can be seen in a detail of an example dated 1720–40.

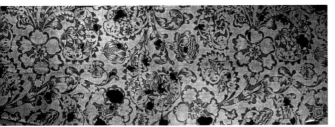

'Indienne' patterns such as this were both block printed and copperplate printed in northern Europe between 1650 and 1700. The black ink patterns were essentially lively outlines, which were sometimes filled in or coloured over by hand painting with mordants for a golden-yellow or a red dye.

subcontinent with the chartering of the English East India Company (EIC), which established its first warehouses at Surat within a decade and had gained landing rights along the Coromandel Coast by 1611.

Until the 1660s the majority of calicos brought to Europe were of the more modest types, and it was only in 1669 that cottons finally surpassed pepper as the largest category of EIC imports. Thereafter the *kalamkari* and *pintados* were quick to inspire northern printers; eye-witness reports of Indian techniques written in 1680 and 1688 (in French and Dutch respectively) aided this process. Although the development of western calico printing remains uncertain, it is clear that between about 1650 and 1700 some European printers adapted the Indian method of pattern-dyeing to their established means of printing by making mordants sufficiently 'gummy' to adhere to blocks, thus eliminating the laborious process of hand-painting of mordants. The first English patent for 'the only true way of East India printing and staynning' of calicos was granted to William Sherwin of West Ham near London in 1676. (The patent is now lost, but is recorded by Peter Floud and other historians.) Sherwin, like the French playing-card maker recorded in 1648 as a printer of calicos, was most probably originally a paper printer, a trade in which gum-thickening of inks was already practiced. Although always assumed to refer to block printing, there is ample evidence that copperplate printers were instrumental in the early attempts to print colour-fast dyes on cloth. However, little is known about English printed cottons until the mid-eighteenth century, since few dated samples survive. Those that do show that at first only the 'madder style' had been mastered: pinks, reds, purples, browns and blacks were combined, but no blues were incorporated into 'chintz' patterns until about 1730, when a means of quickly-brushing (or 'pencilling') indigo was perfected and, not long afterwards, the use of ground indigo suspended in a paste. The latter allowed cloths thus printed to be immersed first in a bath of lime to dissolve the indigo, and then in one of ferrous sulphate to develop ('reduce') its colour. By the 1730s, then, English printers had perfected methods of imitating Indian chintzes, substituting simpler and speedier paper-printers' techniques for the ancient practice of hand-painting.

Until 1722 English printers had worked with the imported Indian plain cotton cloths exempted from a 1701 ban (enacted in 1700 as a result of protests from woollen and silk weavers) on the importation of all 'wrought' silks and painted or printed calicos, whether Indian, Persian or Chinese. Home production of printed calicos was given a boost by this prohibition. Then, in 1721, further protests from the wool and silk sector were rewarded with a ban on the printing of all-cotton cloths except for export, as well as their use in Britain after 1722. One result was that from 1701 until all bans were lifted in 1774, the American colonies became the principal recipients of both East India Company imports and English imitations, though some ships deposited their 'contraband' cloths in northern British ports. In addition, as Pamela Clabburn has noted, printed calicos and other Indian goods could be obtained from Holland. A second result may well have been the apparent increase in the making of

Wooden rollers were used to emboss uncoloured patterns on cloth at least as early as the 1660s, but their use for one-colour printing was not perfected until the 1780s. It took about 20 years before the technology became widespread. After several improvements, by 1830 many three-colour roller printing machines were in operation in Lancashire. Once rollers were engraved, they were used for as many thousands of metres of cloth as possible. Since blocks could be used for many decades, both features contributed to the longevity of many designs.

patchwork coverlets and quilts. A set of hangings dated 1708 (Levens Hall, Westmorland) is the earliest evidence in England of true patchwork, arranged into a deliberate pattern rather than patched solely for repair, which was an ancient practice. After 1722, however, patchworked furnishings had the advantage of being far less likely than clothing to attract the £5 fine for using printed or dyed calico; in addition, they provided a use for quantities of printed all-cotton calico gowns that could no longer be worn. This was the case for any washable fabric, so when Fanny Boscawen (see Saumarez Smith) recorded in 1748 that 'I bestow [to bed or window hangings in the house at South Audley Street, London] my old chintz gowns as fast as they wear out', she may equally have meant contraband chintz – since her husband was Admiral Edward Boscawen and had easy access to these – or home-produced printed fustian.

Dating from 1750–75, white ground all-cotton chintzes such as this were made in India especially to suit European tastes. By this period London printers were also able to produce comparable effects on Lancashire fustian cloths made with a linen warp and a cotton weft.

The third and major result of early eighteenth-century legislation was that, for the home trade, British calico printers turned to those cloths called fustians, formerly with a textured surface but now made as flat as possible to accommodate printers' needs. The use of fustians as print-cloths was validated by a further act of Parliament in 1736, dubbed the Manchester Act, no doubt because smooth fustians were the speciality of Blackburn and surrounding areas and handled by the growing number of Manchester textile merchants. By about 1750 it was said that a thousand rolls of new-style fustians a week were being sent to London to be bleached and printed there. Many throughout this period had designs related to those seen on dress silks (and the bleached white grounds and glazed finish served to heighten this comparison). Old-style fustians – the so-called 'Manchester velvets' (cotton velvets) – were already printed in Lancashire, and at the same time calico printing as practiced in London began to be taken up in Lancashire as well. English printers had also benefited northern weavers with this substitution of linen-warp, cotton-weft cloths for the all-cotton fabrics of India. Linen spinners were similarly aided because, unlike Indian hand-spinners, westerners could not produce a cotton yarn strong enough for a warp.

It was only in the late 1820s that printing machines could produce a full-colour chintz. This example of the period is 'union' or 'mule' printed, meaning that the machine had an engraved copper roller printing the mordant for all the red-brown shades, plus two raised wooden rollers to supply the yellow and blue.

Having dominated English calico printing for a century, London in the 1770s gave way to Lancashire as the source of the next phase of developments. Among other innovations, those of greatest impact for printers were Richard Arkwright's water-powered spinning mill (established in 1771 with spinning frames he had patented in 1769), Samuel Crompton's spinning mule (patented in 1779 and within two years adapted for James Watt's 1769 invention of steam engines), Thomas Bell's engraved roller printing machine of 1783–4, and Edmund Cartwright's power loom, 1787. The machine spinners provided a plentiful supply of cotton yarns strong enough for warps (and the mule's were also very fine) and the looms produced a ready supply of print-cloth, the best of which were called 'percale', after the *percalla* once obtained from the Coromandel Coast, particularly from the weavers of Madras and Golconda. It took some two or more decades for the industrial methods to coalesce, but by the later 1820s three-colour, all-cotton, entirely machine-made British printed calicos were widely available. Nevertheless, additional colours were still hand-blocked and many high-quality furnishing chintzes continued to be entirely hand-printed. In fact, these

While the flowers in the previous illustration were typical of middle class gardens of the mid-1800s, the rhododendrons depicted in this design of July 1869 for a hand-block printed chintz were exotic blooms then associated with country houses and large conservatories. The pattern is also much bigger. Like Brodsworth's 'Champion Chintz', 'Rhododendron' was originally printed by Clarkson & Turner for Daniel Walters & Sons, who supplied it to customers including Lapworths; they in turn are known to have used both chintzes in Castle Howard. Today the pattern is supplied by Warner Fabrics.

RIGHT: During the 1930s 'modern' chintzes were boldly drawn and often incorporated unusual motifs such as seen on the right in 'Cactus'. Both designs were created by Lewis Jones of the Silver Studio, London, in 1937 (left) and 1938 (right). They were hand-screen printed by Warner & Sons, which printed their own screens and blocks from 1932–40.

The printing of more innovative chintzes was made possible by introduction of hand-screen printing on a commercial scale in the early 1930s. The screens were inexpensive to make (unlike rollers for machines or blocks for hand-printing) and as a result smaller amounts could be printed to cater to more adventurous tastes.

often flamboyant prints now garnered considerable cachet as their significantly greater cost set them apart from machine-printed cottons: their repeats became larger, their colours richer and more numerous and some 30 or more blocks might be needed to print one design. The glazed varieties were also more expensive to maintain, since the glazing had to be renewed periodically.

The many-coloured, hand-printed, smooth-as-paper chintz was a luxury by the late 1860s, when the cotton shortage caused by the American Civil War had made the use of waste-yarns, mixed-fibre cloths and unglazed textured cloths (cretonnes) a necessity for many. During the same decade the removal of the high tariff barriers between France and Britain increased the exchange of both designs and finished cloths between these two countries, and English calico printers were thereafter often accused of being too dependent upon French designers. In truth, few printers then or before had originated their own designs; the now-reduced production of chintzes continued to rely instead on commissions from wholesale fabric firms, whose specialist clients – furniture makers and interior decorators – up until about 1940 maintained the use of both revived and newly designed chintzes in the face

of successive avant garde tastes and design critics alike. Thereafter, despite a century of developments in synthetic dyes and the introduction of hand-screen printing in the 1930s – followed by rotary screen printing in the 1950s – it was the Victorian block-printed chintz style that became a perennial, having adapted to its new environment as graciously as had the rhododendrons, azaleas, peonies, orchids and other once-exotic imported flowering plants that graced many Victorian gardens and hothouses and inspired so many designs.

Until the development of hand-screen printing, a long-standing compromise between the high cost of block printing and inexpensive roller printing was the combination of the two, and this was how 'Honeysuckle' was first produced in about 1890 for Warner & Sons. Its arrangement into an informal meander suited Art Nouveau trends and it was a popular design, ordered by Lloyds, Lapworths and Waring & Gillow for several clients, including Nostell Priory and Harewood House, both in Yorkshire. 'Honeysuckle' has been supplied by Warners to Colefax & Fowler since 1923.

The use of chintz

④

From 1500 to 1600, just as Europeans were becoming exposed at first hand to the rich textile tradition of the Indian subcontinent, western modes of living were also undergoing substantial changes. Residences designed for both private luxuries and public entertaining began to replace the castles and fortified manor houses that typified the previous unsettled era. Multi-purpose portable furniture and textile hangings began their gradual transition towards objects with well-defined roles within interiors. Rooms themselves emerged with specific functions, among them – importantly for chintzes – the bedroom. At the same time, decoration developed in forms we would recognise today: across a broadening swathe of society, plate, glass, ceramics, cutlery and textiles now served as much for ornament as for use. Under the sway of Mannerism (the Italian movement that transformed the fine and decorative arts across Europe during this century), the taste for opulence, strong contrasts, vivid effects and the display of 'curiosities' transformed sober interiors into diverse expressions of power, privilege or aspiration, depending on what their owners could obtain. Within this context, it is easy to understand the wonder of Indian chintzes, Mannerist even to the extent of their incorporation of twisted forms and broken lines. And not only were they ornamental, but these richly coloured cottons were also washable, a feature that was to favour their use in a world increasingly concerned with comfort and cleanliness.

The riches of the 'orient' – a term embracing all of the lands east of the Mediterranean – had long been known to the west. However, new in this era was their transport to Europe by sea rather than overland, as well as the growing dominance of westerners in these shipping trades. The Portuguese led the way, supplying northern Europe via Dutch ships until 1594, when Lisbon's port was closed by Spain. Holland, at war with Spain, retaliated by seizing Portuguese-held parts of Java and, with this, the monopoly of the spice trade. English interest in eastward sea routes came only after they had expended considerable efforts to find westward passages to the Spice Islands. Although Sir Francis Drake succeeded in a westward circumnavigation of the globe in 1577–80, it was privateers (officially sanctioned 'pirates' such as Sir Walter Raleigh) who laid the splendours of the East before the London court with their capture in 1592 of the 1600-ton Portuguese

In this detail of *Sir Thomas Aston at his Wife's Deathbed* painted by John Souch in 1635, Aston's celestial globe stands upon a chintz table cover, or 'carpet'. It is thought to be a painted cotton from Masulipatam. In Aston's day, both objects equally would have suggested a man with worldly mercantile interests (other details imply he was a navigator or surveyor) and an eye for the 'latest thing'.

The 'calico carpets' recorded in English inventories may well have resembled this 1640s' cotton from India's Golconda region. Entirely hand painted with resists and mordants for a full range of dyes, its imagery includes many Persian features. Carpets of all types were rarities in Europe at this time and were generally used on tables or hung on the wall.

carrack, the *Madre de Dios*. Principal among the 900 tons of seized merchandise were 'spices, drugges, silks, callicos, quilts, carpets and colours... The calicos were book-calicos, calico launes [lawns], broad white calicos, fine starched calicos, course white calico, browne broad calicos, browne course calicos. There were also canopies and course diaper-towels, quilts of course sarcenet and of calico, [and] carpets like those of Turkey...'.[1] Once the English East India Company (EIC) was formed eight years later, their lading lists showed a similar predominance of relatively plain cloths for another 40 years or so. Broad calicos – up to three yards wide – were used as bedclothes, while coarse ones went for clothing, in place of more expensive Dutch linens. Other plain materials found their way into grand settings. Hardwick Hall in 1601 had sun-curtains of the thin silk sarsenet (which might be striped, checked, or 'clouded' with pre-dyed – or ikat – spots, all recorded at Ham House and some probably in place in 1640, used as sun-blinds and protective covers not only for beds and furniture but also for wall-hangings). Cockesden, a house associated with the Earls of Leicester, had curtains of green cotton and a cupboard cloth of 'Indyan stuff' in 1610.[2]

Far fewer in number were the *pintados* such as those noted in Surat in 1609 by an EIC factor (in charge of the Indian warehouse, or 'factory') as 'the finest...for quilts and for fine hangings', or the '*chintes*...for hangings in England' commissioned by another factor in 1619. Such cloths were expensive: *pintado* hangings cost £30 in 1630.[3] Judging from the 'six stayned Callico Carpitts' among the 48 listed in the Easton Lodge (Essex) Inventory of 1637, only those entirely covered with embroidery or knotted in true Turkish manner were more costly. The most ornamental of Indian cloths seem largely to have been destined for relatives

From the 1600s into the 1800s, the East India Companies provided detailed descriptions or patterns through their agents for printing in India. This rare surviving example is painted in watercolour and was found in Masulipatam, a major centre of chintz production in Andrha Pradesh. It is dated 1810 on the reverse.

During the 1700s, different sections of the textile trade battled to retain their markets through political means. Agitation against imported chintzes, and later those made in Britain, was led by weavers of wool and 'half-silks', the dress cloths made of silk and worsted. The first were banned in 1701, prompting the printing of imported plain cottons in England. These in turn were also banned in 1722, but the printing of linen-cotton cloths remained legal. All bans came to an end in 1744, not long after mechanised cotton spinning became established in Lancashire. By the 1820s this region had overtaken India as the largest producer of printed cottons in the world.

of EIC employees such as Lady Haversly, who had 'free of freight 2 small cabinets and 10 pieces of calicos sent her by her son-in-law' in 1640.[4] With one piece being some 35–37 yards long, this amount would have easily furnished an entire room, as had become the fashion by the 1630s. They also circulated among those closest to the court. For example, during the same period, Aletheia, wife of the prominent courtier Thomas Howard, 2nd Earl of Arundel (1586–1646), had three rooms in Tart Hall, Westminster, including her own bedroom, hung with Indian painted cottons.[5] By this time, however, the political unrest in England had already turned merchants away from the financial risks involved in dealing with imported indigo, silks and calicos; in 1640 the EIC recorded the latter as 'a dead commodity, neither linen drapers nor others offering reasonable prices for them.'[6]

After a period of floundering trade, the EIC, with Oliver Cromwell's support, was reorganised in 1657. For both the Company and chintzes, however, the real change of fortune occurred with the marriage in 1662 of Charles II to the Portuguese princess, Catherine of Braganza. Her dowry, the richest in Europe, included free trading rights for English ships in the ports of the Portuguese East Indies, Tangiers, Bombay and Brazil (the latter to become an important source of raw cotton for British spinners until American crops overtook this position in the nineteenth century). In the same year renewed orders were sent out to India by the EIC, together with patterns for chintzes; in the following year 'a Chinke' to hang in his wife's study was bought in London's Cornhill by Samuel Pepys, who had watched over Catherine's cash in the days immediately following her arrival.[7] With the transfer of Bombay from the Portuguese completed by 1667 and the EIC empowered to make war and peace in 1676, the floodgates at last opened. EIC orders increased over those of the 1660s five- to six-fold; *palampores* (large panels, usually with elaborate borders surrounding a large one-directional design, often a tree of life) were first noted in 1676 and within four years were so fashionable for bed-hangings that the Company ordered '100 Suits of painted Curtains and vallances of Several Sorts and Prices, ...but none too dear, nor any overmean in regard you know our Poorest people in England lye without any Curtains or Vallances and our richest in Damask...'.[8] Despite her own ill-fortune as a queen, Catherine introduced her native tastes, including two that were to become defining for the English: tea and chintz. By the time she left Whitehall in 1685, not only were the marble walls of her own bathing chamber hung with India stuffs, but 'plenty of these colourful materials were to be seen in every grand house in England.... The 'Calleco Chamber' at Cowdray in 1682 was in no way exceptional.

Shown as displayed at the Victoria & Albert Museum is David Garrick's bedroom furniture, made by Haig and Chippendale in 1771 in chinoiserie style. The *palampore* bed hangings were a gift to Garrick from Calcutta but, being banned at the time, were confiscated. Garrick appealed to the Secretary of the Customs for their return and, in the event, the ban ended in 1774.

From about 1720 until the 1830s, 'furniture checks' and their simpler variant, stripes, were used as often as chintzes as bed-hangings, curtains, loose covers and upholstery. Both initially shared associations with the Indian subcontinent, which gave to English the term 'gingham'. However, after about 1830 when power-machine weaving became widespread, checks became cheaper and until about 1920 were most often found in workers' rural or urban dwellings.

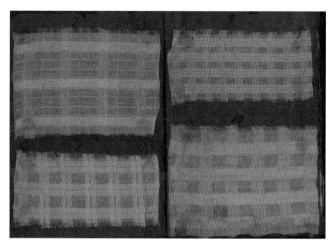

John Bradshaw's 1827 sample book of 'gingham plad' muslins woven by Brown & Villing of Bolton illustrates yet another type of fabric far more readily available as a result of the Industrial Revolution. Such lightweight muslins were woven from the fine machine-spun cotton yarns for which Lancashire became famed. The ready supply of cotton yarns sustained the fashion for under-curtains, or sheers. Whether plain, of lace or embroidered, these often hung beneath chintz curtains, as occurred at Brodsworth.

Not only were the wall-hangings of this room of "painted caleco", but also the window-curtains, the table-covers and the hangings of the bed',[9] as well as the chair-covers and carpet.

Since the fashion for chintz was equally prevalent in the Netherlands, Denmark and France (which had their own East India companies from 1602, 1616 and 1664 respectively), the taste for 'oriental' goods was maintained until 1714 by succeeding Stuart monarchs: James II, William III and Mary II, all of whom had strong connections with those countries, and Anne, whose husband was Prince George of Denmark. Dutch influence was especially marked during the reign of William and Mary (1689–1702); at both Hampton Court Palace and Windsor the Queen's bed was covered in chintz.

Despite the ban on imported Indian printed or painted cottons, which took effect in 1701, these continued in circulation as contraband, supplemented by trade goods from China whose ports opened to the English in 1699. By this date, full-colour chintzes were firmly associated with beds and their en suite decor; printed calicos (which in this period may well have denoted an unglazed 'demi-chintz', more limited in palette) were avidly sought for clothing. The outcry against such cottons was already reaching fever pitch before the end of Queen Anne's reign, but it was only after the accession of the Hanoverian king, George I (1714–27) that all use of these was banned. From 1722 until 1774, printed fustians provided a legal alternative, as did painted Indian and Chinese silks (being neither 'wrought' – that is, embroidered or pattern-woven – nor calicos), yet other factors reduced the demand for painted and printed cloths within interiors of this period.

Although they and their origins were not forgotten – as indicated by the generic name for printed cottons and linens in French, *indiennes* – the introduction of competing goods offered ample distraction. Among these were English-made damasks and more elaborate silks, still something of a novelty in 1714, and German (and then English-made) 'furniture checks'. The latter were widely used in both fixed and loose upholstering on beds and, in particular, the burgeoning range of seat furniture that characterises this period. The apparent simplicity of checked fustians belies their exotic origins, which can be traced back to checked and striped Indian sarcenets and their lighter variants, persians, as well as to ginghams (from the Tamil *kindam*) and Gujarati 'Cambay cloths' and their close relatives, *siamoises*. The latter were originally silk warp/cotton weft stripes and checks woven in France from the 1680s in imitation of Siamese (Thai) cloths, themselves often originating from Gujarat. *Siamoise* became the ubiquitous French furnishing fabric after about 1720, when it was woven with linen in place of silk. In England, the production of linen and cotton furniture checks, woven in districts around Manchester, may well have increased with the prohibition of EIC silks, since their prices were comparable and far lower than those of English-made silks.

Furniture checks and stripes remained popular into the 1830s, but increasingly after 1775 English all-cotton chintzes encroached on their domain. Patterns designed specifically for use on newly fashionable, light-weight, less formal seating were available by the 1780s and a marked feature of surviving designs and cloths from the mid-1790s until the 1820s. During the same period bedrooms ceased to be reception rooms. Informal entertaining moved into the drawing room, itself a feature new in the many houses designed for the rising middle classes. Chintzes moved too, enjoying this 40–50 year period of popularity as both fixed and loose upholstery and as the basis for increasingly elaborate window treatments. History then repeated itself when a flood of less expensive, Jacquard-woven cloths became available in the 1830s. Yet in the ensuing delight in revivals, which favoured boldly-patterned woven cloths whether gothic or neo-renaissance in inspiration, floral chintzes survived. Many from the 1830s onwards had designs adapted from those of about 1775–95. Some, it seems, also carried undertones of the Stuart dynasty, whose interiors were to inspire the 'medieval' and 'Queen Anne' styles promoted by such diverse decorators as the Craces, Charles Eastlake and William Morris, whose firm's first three fabrics were hand-printed in about 1868 at Bannister Hall, Lancashire, using blocks of the 1830s with decidedly 'Indian' designs. Many similar designs were reprinted in subsequent years, but all were too late to aid the ailing EIC, which ceased trading in 1857, having already become preoccupied with the politics of the subcontinent.

The 'Queen of Scots' bedroom at Chatsworth was decorated *en suite* (that is, with matching fabrics throughout) in 1830. The chintz, hand-block printed to order at Charles Swainson & Company, Bannister Hall, incorporates a border along the sides and, for the bed and window curtains, at precisely measured points across the cloth to create a bottom border. Although very much of its time, the light 'sprinkling' of florals in the chintz design harks back to patterns of two centuries earlier.

Thereafter, block- and machine-printed chintzes became the staple of interior decorators and the furnishing fabric wholesale firms who supplied both decorators and other clientele, including the many new department stores that emerged in the later nineteenth century. In general, the latter tended to stock only the roller-printed variety, with their designs by the turn of the century often given a fashionable 'neo-regency' twist through the incorporation of stripes, or rendered 'oriental' with flowers such as chrysanthemums in embrowned colours. In an ironic turn of events, many traditionally-styled hand-prints were promoted by Americans, whose forebears had purchased so many eighteenth-century EIC imports and, later, English chintzes. Some were heiresses who married British aristocrats and consolidated the English country house style; others were taste-makers such as Elsie de Wolfe and her younger compatriot, Dorothy Draper, who between them had thousands of yards of cloth shipped to the United States

The use of a chintz for fixed upholstery (rather than for washable loose covers) as much as for elaborate bed draperies and festoons at the window, reinforced the grandeur of an *en suite* scheme. By the 1830s such formality was a last vestige of the use of bedrooms as reception rooms in country houses.

After the First World War, 'tea and chintz' had comforting nostalgic connotations, here epitomised by a photograph of Miss Penelope Chetwode and her horse taking tea with Lord Berners at Faringdon House, Berkshire. The elegantly ill-fitting loose covers are of 'Camellia' chintz, first printed for Warners in 1927–32. Providing a fashionable note to the room are its colours (a butter yellow ground, stippled by roller printing to create a subtle texture) and the simplified rendering of a mid-nineteenth-century camellia chintz in hand-blocked muted shades of brown and green, with delicately stippled flower heads.

A classic chintz, 'Maryport' has been available from Warners since the late 1800s, at which time the design was also handwoven. During the 1930s and 1940s they supplied it as a hand-block print to Dorothy Draper of New York, who in 1944 illustrated it as loose covers and on a four-poster bed in *Decorating is Fun!* It has since then been continued as a screen printed.

between about 1910 and 1940; notably, there was Nancy Tree, who after World War II purchased the London decorating firm Sybil Colefax Ltd from Lady Colefax[10] (see 'Honeysuckle' illustration in chapter 3). From the 1860s onwards, records of these and other commissions survive in only a handful of country houses, such as Brodsworth Hall, and a few archives. One, the Warner Archive, holds evidence of commissions given by several decorating firms to both Daniel Walters and Warner & Sons (which purchased Walter's designs and mill in 1895); among these are Lapworth orders for other Yorkshire houses, including Castle Howard (see 'Rhododendron' illustration in chapter 3), Temple Newsam and Nostell Priory, several of which remain available today. [11]

Notes

1 See entry for Sir Walter Raleigh in Further Reading chapter 4

2 See entries for Peter Thornton and Florence Montgomery in Further Reading chapter 4

3 See entry for John Irwin and Katherine B Brett in Further Reading chapter 3, pp3–4

4 See entry for Ethel B Sainsbury in Further Reading chapter 4; see also entry for Pamela Clabburn in Further Reading chapter 3, p125, regarding *pintado* bed curtains described as 'old' in 1620

5 Tart Hall also contained en suite decoration in plaid, of pertinence to Victorian revivals of this fashion; see entry for Lionel Cust in Further Reading chapter 4

6 See entry for Ethel B Sainsbury in Further Reading chapter 4, p45

7 See entry for Robert Latham and William Matthews in Further Reading chapter 4; for the chintz purchase see 5 September 1663, p410

8 *India Office Archives, Letter Book VII*, p136; Irwin notes that in 1695–6 the EIC records indicate that 40,000 *palampores* were imported, half of which were large and the remainder divided equally between medium and small sizes

9 See entry for Peter Thornton in Further Reading chapter 4

10 See entry for Mary Schoeser and Celia Rufey in Further Reading chapter 4

11 This information kindly provided by Sue Kerry, Archivist, The Warner Archive

FURTHER READING

This reading list is arranged by chapter since the titles relate to the subject matter of the individual chapters; where the reading list for chapters 3 and 4 gives page references, they relate to specific points made in the text.

Introduction
Carr-Whitworth, C, 1995, rev edn 2000, *Brodsworth Hall*, London, English Heritage
Carr-Whitworth, C, 1999, Fleeting images: the Brodsworth Hall photograph collection, *Collections Review*, 2, 109–12
Girouard, M, 1978, *Life in the English Country House*, New Haven & London, Yale University Press
Girouard, M, 1979, *The Victorian Country House*. New Haven & London, Yale University Press

Chapter 1
Collections Review, 1, 1997, 40, for details of the Flint watercolour (p12)
Sweet, M, 2001, *Inventing the Victorians*, London, Faber & Faber
Thornton, P, 1984, *Authentic Decor: the Domestic Interior 1620–1920*, London, Weidenfeld & Nicolson
Victoria and Albert Museum, 1960, *Catalogue of a Loan Exhibition of Chintz: English Printed Furnishing Fabrics from their Origins until the Present Day*, London, V&A

Chapter 2
Allfrey, M, 1999, Brodsworth Hall: the preservation of a country house, in G Chitty & D Baker (eds), *Managing Historic Sites and Buildings: Reconciling Presentation and Conservation*, London, Routledge, 115–27
Barty-King, H, 1992, *Maples Fine Furnishers: A Household Word for 150 Years 1841–1991*, London, Quiller Press
Bury, H, 1981, *A Choice of Design, 1850–1980: Fabrics by Warner and Son Limited*, Exhibition catalogue, Purley, Purley Press
Hall, M, 1995, Brodsworth Hall, Yorkshire, *Country Life*, 29 June, 60–5
Jackson, L, 2002, *20th-Century Pattern Design: Textile and Wallpaper Pioneers*, London, Mitchell Beazley
Stevens, C, 2001, Evidence from artefacts and archives: researching the textile furnishings of a Victorian bedroom at Brodsworth Hall, in K Gill & D Eastop (eds), *Upholstery Conservation: Principles and Practice*, Oxford, Butterworth-Heinemann, 144–73
Victoria and Albert Museum, 1970, *A Century of Warners Fabrics, 1870–1970*, London, V&A

Chapter 3
Brédif, Josette, 1989, *Toiles de Jouy: Classic Printed Textiles from France 1760–1843*, London, Thames & Hudson, 16
Clabburn, Pamela, 1988, *The National Trust Book of Furnishing Textiles*, London, Viking, 41, 247
Floud, Peter, 1960, The Origins of English Calico Printing, *The Journal of the Society of Dyers and Colourists*, 76 (May), 275
Gittinger, Mattiebelle, 1982, *Master Dyers to the World: Technique and Trade in Early Indian Dyed Cotton Textiles*,

The Textile Museum, Washington DC
Guy, John, 1998, *Woven Cargoes: Indian Textiles in the East*, London, Thames & Hudson, 7–36
Irwin, John, & Brett, Katharine B, 1970, *Origins of Chintz*, London, V&A
Lemire, Beverley, 2003, Domesticating the Exotic: Floral Culture and the East India Calico Trade with England, *c*1600–1800, *Textile: the Journal of Cloth and Culture*, **I/1** (March), 62–85
Rose, Mary (ed), 1996, *The Lancashire Cotton Industry: a History since 1700*, Preston, Lancashire County Books
Saumarez Smith, Charles, 1993, *Eighteenth-Century Decoration: Design and the Domestic Interior in England*, New York, Harry N Abrams, 48, 216
Schoeser, Mary, 2002, The Mystery of the Printed Hankie, in Mary Schoeser & Christine Boydell (eds), *Disentangling Textiles: Techniques for the Study of Designed Objects*, London, Middlesex University Press, 13–22
Schoeser, Mary, 2003, *World Textiles, a Concise History*, London, Thames & Hudson, ch 7

Chapter 4
Cust, Lionel, 1911, Notes on the collections formed by Thomas Howard, Earl of Arundel and Surrey, KG, *Burlington Magazine*, pt II, 97–100, 233–6, and pt IV, 341–3
Latham, Thomas, & Matthews, William (eds), 1995, 2000, *The Diary of Samuel Pepys: a New and Complete Transcription*, vols 3–4, 1662–3, London, HarperCollins
Montgomery, Florence, 1984, *Textiles in America 1650–1870*, London & New York, W W Norton & Co, 339
Raleigh, Sir Walter, A true report… in Richard Hakluyt, *The Principall Navigations, Voiages and Discoveries of the English Nation…*, Glasgow, James MacLehose & Sons, 1903, 116–17
Sainsbury, Ethel B, 1907–38, *A Calendar of the Court Minutes, etc, of the East India Company 1640–1643*, Oxford, Clarendon Press, 18
Schoeser, Mary, & Rufey, Celia, 1989, *English and American Textiles from 1790 to the Present*, London & New York, Thames & Hudson, 145–6, 174–6, 233
Thornton, Peter, 1978, *Seventeenth-century Interior Decoration in England, Holland and France*, New Haven & London, Yale University Press, 116

Glossary
Trench, Lucy (ed), 2000, *Materials & Techniques in the Decorative Arts: an illustrated dictionary*, London, John Murray

GLOSSARY

BROCATELLE: a fabric related to damask but with raised areas created by incorporating more warp threads than can lie together in one plane. The warps are often divided into two sets, one of which remains unseen at the back and is often linen; the primary warp and weft are usually silk.

CREWELWORK: embroidery employing crewel (worsted) threads on fustian in, typically, a stem stitch, which is also called crewel stitch as a result. The term is especially associated with the designs of *c*1650-1710 with large leaf or tree-of-life patterns influenced by Indian chintzes.

DAMASK: a fabric, usually of a single colour, with a design that appears to be two-toned because light reflects off the surface of two different weave structures, typically a satin (which is smooth) and a twill (which has a diagonal texture).

DIMITY: a firmly-woven cotton cloth with a self-coloured pattern, usually a textured stripe or a diamond-shaped spot.

FUSTIAN: formerly a richly-surfaced cloth such as corduroy, made with a linen warp and a cotton weft; 'new' fustian became common in the 1720s. It used the same fibres but was entirely flat to make it more suitable for printing.

IKAT: a Malay/Indonesian word for patterns created by resist-dyeing specific areas of the warp prior to weaving. An ancient technique also widely used on the Indian subcontinent, it creates a 'shadowy' edge around motifs. In about 1837 a method of mechanically pre-printing the warps was developed and this is often called 'shadow printing' and sometimes 'chiné'.

REP: a horizontally ribbed fabric made in a plain weave with a fine warp and a thicker, concealed, weft.

UTRECHT VELVET: a strong, thick upholstery velvet with a pattern created by crushing some of the pile with hot metal blocks or engraved cylinders. The latter process was patented in France in 1838.

WARP: in weaving, the longitudinal threads that are attached to the loom and manipulated up or down to create an opening for the passage of a weft thread.

ACKNOWLEDGEMENTS

The authors and English Heritage have many debts of gratitude in the research of the Brodsworth Hall chintz collection and in the publication of this book. Thanks are owed to the archival and curatorial staff at the Stead McAlpin Archive, Carlisle, part of the John Lewis Partnership; the Warner Archive, Milton Keynes, and its archivist, Sue Kerry; the Department of Textiles and Dress at the Victoria and Albert Museum, London; the Musée de L'Impression sur Étoffes, Mulhouse, France; the Colour Museum, Bradford; Temple Newsam, Leeds; Nostell Priory, Wakefield; Harewood House, Leeds; the Sanderson and Son Design Archive, Uxbridge; Ramm, Son and Crocker, Chelsea Harbour, London; The Textile Conservation Centre, Winchester; A T Cronin, London; and Textile Research in Archaeology, York. We are also indebted to John Miners, James Cartland, and Dorian Church. Full archive references and inventory numbers have not been given in the text but are available on request.

All the illustrations, with the exception of those listed below, are copyright English Heritage or English Heritage.NMR. Some of the English Heritage photographs were commissioned for the chintz exhibition at Brodsworth Hall and taken by Keith Paisley, including the cover image; details are available on request.

Pages 32, 38 bottom left and 39 top right copyright © V&A Images/V&A Museum; page 37 copyright © Manchester Art Gallery, UK/Bridgeman Art Library; page 40 top left copyright © Bolton Museum & Art Gallery; page 38 top left copyright © Cincinnati Art Museum; pages 33 bottom right, 34 bottom left and 35 top right copyright © Temple Newsam House, Roger Warner Collections; pages 33 top right, 34 top left, 35 bottom right, all images on page 36 and 42 bottom left copyright © the Warner Archive; page 41 top right copyright © The Devonshire Collection, Chatsworth, reproduced by permission of the Duke of Devonshire and the Chatsworth Settlement Trustees; page 42 top right copyright © the estate of Robert Heber-Percy Esq